T-MINUS
the race to the moon

jim OTTAVIANI   zander CANNON   kevin CANNON

Aladdin

New York   London   Toronto   Sydney

This book is a work of historical fiction. Any references to historical events, real people, or real locales are used fictitiously. Other names, characters, places, and incidents are the product of the author's imagination, and any resemblance to actual events or locales or persons, living or dead, is entirely coincidental.

ALADDIN

An imprint of Simon & Schuster Children's Publishing Division
1230 Avenue of the Americas, New York, NY 10020
Text copyright © 2009 by Jim Ottaviani
Illustrations copyright © 2009 by Zander Cannon and Kevin Cannon
All rights reserved, including the right of reproduction in whole or in part in any form.
ALADDIN and related logo are registered trademarks of Simon & Schuster, Inc.
Designed by Zander Cannon and Kevin Cannon
Manufactured in the United States of America
First Aladdin edition May 2009
10 9 8 7 6 5 4 3 2 1
Library of Congress Control Number 2009920999
ISBN: 978-1-4169-8682-9 (hc)
ISBN: 978-1-4169-4960-2 (pbk)

To my parents, who let me stay up past my bedtime to watch the first humans walk around on another world.
—Jim Ottaviani

To Julie and Jin-Seo
—Zander Cannon

For R. A.
—Kevin Cannon

Thanks to Kevin, Zander, Liesa, the folks at NASA, the astronauts who answered questions, and everyone who helped make this book possible (not quite 400,000, but close).—J. O.

The astronauts may be famous for going to the moon, but it took tens of thousands of people working behind the scenes to get them there. Likewise, T-Minus wouldn't exist without many talented people working behind the scenes. Jim Ottaviani wrote a fantastic script, but he also patiently answered our many artistic and reference questions in the form of late-night e-mails. It has been a thrill and an honor to work on another book with Jim, and if our luck holds out, this will be the second of many more to come. Liesa Abrams believed in this project from the start, and, with the help of her crack team at Aladdin, produced the gorgeous book you're now holding. Bob Mecoy, our agent, and Matt Madden, our editor, have been encouraging, insightful, and even dogged (when necessary) during this project's long and exciting journey. We also owe thanks to the photographers, writers, website producers, and museum curators whose enthusiasm for the space race shines through in their work and who have indirectly helped this extremely research-heavy book come to fruition. And finally, we'd like to thank our friends and family for being with us as we slowly counted down to T-minus 0.—Z. C. and K. C.

1

R-7 Semyorka
May 15, 1957
T-Minus 12 Years
Flight duration:
20 seconds

DESIGN BUREAU 1, SCIENTIFIC-RESEARCH INSTITUTE NO. 88, DEPARTMENT NO. 3. = The Russian equivalent of NASA.

UNSUCCESSFUL

THEY DID EVERYTHING BUT LICK IT TO SEE HOW IT **TASTED**.

SO IT WENT ...WELL?

VERY WELL ...SO FAR.

LET US GO RESCUE THE COMPUTERS FROM THE POLITICIANS.

PREMIER KHRUSHCHEV --

-- IF YOU WOULD STEP THIS WAY, THERE ARE OTHER THINGS TO SEE.

OUR COMPUTERS SHOULD REALLY GET BACK TO WORK.

That's right -- in 1950s Russia, a **"COMPUTER"** was a person! (Usually a woman.)

THANK YOU, CHIEF DESIGNER.

YOU'RE WELCOME. NOW, PLEASE GET BACK TO WORK.

THOSE CALCULATIONS ARE CRITICAL, AFTER ALL!

...NOW, **THIS** SPUTNIK IS ONLY THE **PROTOTYPE**, PREMIER KHRUSHCHEV.

BUT I ASSURE YOU, IT WILL BE IN A **MUSEUM** ONE DAY.

AND THE REAL THING...

...IT MUST SHINE SO THEY WILL SEE IT FROM EARTH WHEN IT PASSES OVERHEAD.

"THEY"? THE AMERICANS?

YES, THE AMERICANS.

AND THE POLITICIANS HERE, AT THE KREMLIN.

THEY APPARENTLY GROW BORED OF ROCKETS...

Jupiter AM-1A
March 1, 1957
T-Minus 12 Years
Flight duration:
7.4 seconds

3

WELL, THAT'S WHAT I HEARD. THE RUSSKIES, THEY --

AH, DON'T YOU BELIEVE IT. IF OUR BOY VON BRAUN CAN'T EVEN GET HIS **JUPITER ROCKET** TO LAUNCH, HOW CAN THE RUSSKIES PUT UP A **SATELLITE**?

IT'S JUST A MATTER OF TIME, FELLAS.

ALL THE ATTENTION IS BECAUSE IT'S THE INTERNATIONAL GEOPHYSICAL YEAR, THAT'S ALL.

INTERNATIONAL GEOPHYSICAL YEAR = IGY = 1957-1958 — A year when scientists around the world agreed to study the Earth, from pole to pole.

A MADE-UP THING -- HECK!

IT'S NOT EVEN A YEAR. IT'S A YEAR AND A HALF.

HA HA HA HA HA HA HA HA

IT'S TRUE -- the IGY was eighteen months long. Those crazy scientists...

WHAT DO YOU THINK, C.C.?

'BOUT WHAT -- ROCKETS? SATELLITES?

THIS IS WHAT I THINK: WHY DON'T WE PUT A **MAN** ON TOP O' ONE OF 'EM?

HA HA HA HA HA HA HA HA HA HA HA HA HA HA HA HA HA HA HA HA HA

HA HA HA HA HA HA

6

UNSUCCESSFUL

Jupiter AM-1B
April 26, 1957
T-Minus 12 Years
Flight duration:
93 seconds

The real **SPUTNIK 1,** not the model, weighed 184 lb.

THE R-7 ROCKET:
An impressive 100 ft. tall and 280 tons --
but only one successful launch so far.

CHIEF?

CHIEF? WHAT'S THE **PLAN?**

WELL, FUTURE MISSIONS WILL HAVE **ANIMALS** -- MAYBE A **DOG** -- AND THEN AFTER THAT WE GO TO...

AH, YOU MEAN TODAY.

START THE **COUNTDOWN.**

WE'RE ALREADY 17 DAYS LATE FOR TSIOLKOVSKY'S 100TH BIRTHDAY AS IT IS.

KONSTANTIN, I'VE BEEN STANDING HERE FOR FIFTEEN MINUTES. COME TO LUNCH!

PAPA!

TA-DA!

EH?

PAPA!

PAPA!

BUT VAVARA—I THINK VERNE'S CALCULATIONS ARE CORRECT!

PAPA!

PAPA!

I'LL EAT LATER!

Everybody's shouting because Tsiolkovsky was deaf.

NOW... "TO GO TO THE MOON..."

GROAN.

"...THE CANNON OUGHT TO BE PLANTED IN A COUNTRY SITUATED BETWEEN 0° AND 28° OF N. OR S. LATITUDE."

AND IF VERNE'S CORRECT...

... THIS IS AWFUL.

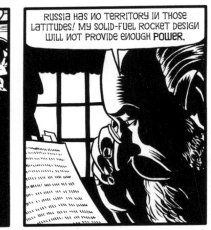

RUSSIA HAS NO TERRITORY IN THOSE LATITUDES! MY SOLID-FUEL ROCKET DESIGN WILL NOT PROVIDE ENOUGH POWER.

"SO...MORE POWERFUL, LIQUID-FUEL ROCKETS, THEN."

T-MINUS 39 YEARS

Before becoming president, Eisenhower was Supreme Allied Commander in Europe at the end of World War II.

GULAG = Russian prison

The Chief Designer's looking at the A4-Fibel, the V-2 rocket launch manual for German soldiers. It had cartoons on most pages.

OKAY...

I THINK THAT'S THE WAY IT'S GOT TO BE.

WHAT I MEAN IS, THAT ORIGINAL DESIGN OF YOURS IS ONLY ABOUT **HALF** RIGHT.

WE NEED TO MAKE THE BOTTOM OF THE CAPSULE REALLY **BLUNT**, AND COME IN BACK END **FIRST**.

THESE THINGS GOTTA GO UP FAST, BUT COME DOWN REAL SLOW, OR WE'LL HAVE OURSELVES BARBECUED **ASTRONAUT**.

VON BRAUN'S V-2 ROCKETS WERE DESIGNED TO DO MAXIMUM DAMAGE, SO IT DIDN'T MATTER IF THEY CAME DOWN BURNING HOT.

BUT IF WE WANT TO LAND SAFELY, WELL ...

THERE'S NO METAL IN THE WORLD THAT CAN CARRY OFF THAT KIND OF HEAT.

DON'T NEED TO BE METAL.

SURE. **SURE!**

A LAYER OF **GAS** WOULD INSULATE IT AND PROTECT WHOEVER ... WHATEVER ... IS INSIDE THE CAPSULE.

Max is right: a **LAYER OF GAS** would absorb almost **90%** of the heat!

AND THE METALLURGY BOYS WILL COME UP WITH SOMETHING THAT'LL GET US THE REST OF THE WAY.

SO ...

...WORKING HARD THIS WEEKEND, FELLAS?

R-7/Sputnik 2
November 3, 1957
T-Minus 12 Years
Flight duration:
162 days
Laika orbits
the Earth

20

REKLAMA I DEISTVITELNOST = Russian for "Publicity and Reality." The Soviets are making fun of the U.S. public launches...and failures.

UNSUCCESSFUL

E-1 Luna Probe,
1st Attempt: 1958
T-Minus 11 Years
Flight Duration:
93 Seconds

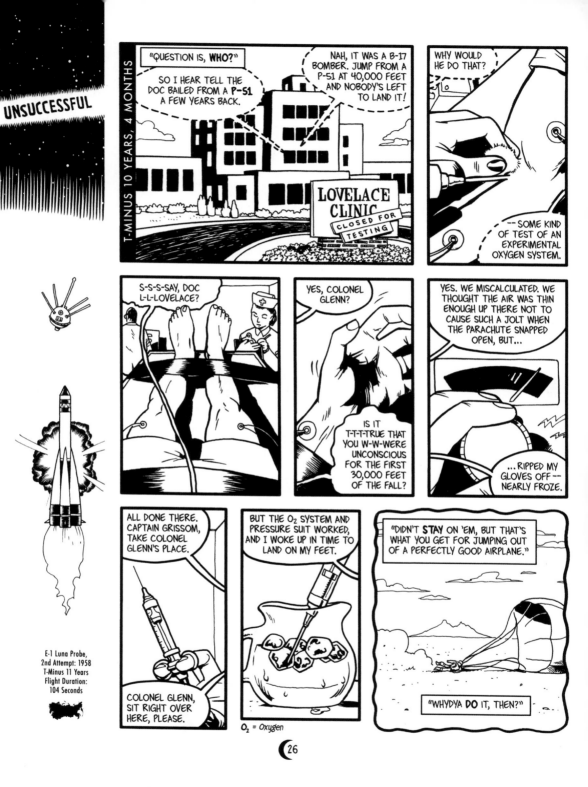

E-1 Luna Probe,
3rd Attempt: 1958
T-Minus 11 Years
Flight Duration:
245 Seconds

28

DOZENS OF TESTS LATER...

SO...

...YOU HAVE ALL PERFORMED VERY WELL INDEED.

SIT DOWN, MY LITTLE EAGLES.

?

I AM KOROLEV.

OF COURSE.

I'M SORRY, YOU WOULDN'T KNOW MY REAL NAME, WOULD YOU?

THEY CALL ME THE CHIEF DESIGNER.

Mercury-Redstone 1:
November 21, 1960
T-Minus 8 Years,
8 Months
Flight Duration:
2 Seconds
Altitude: 4 inches

LAIKA'S life support system broke and she died of heat prostration after only a few Earth orbits.

The RISK is that cosmonauts might get crippling bubbles in their blood ("the bends"), just like deep sea divers who surface too quickly.

VOSTOK = Russian for "East."

ATTITUDE CONTROL isn't about making sure the capsule doesn't mouth off. To an engineer, it means making sure it's oriented correctly relative to the direction it's going.

E-2 Luna Probe: 1959 T-Minus 10 Years, Flight Duration: 33.5 Hours It made it to the moon in a planned crash landing!

In 1959, **LUNA 2** hit the moon and **LUNA 3** took pictures of the far side.

ZVEZDOCHKA'S SPUTNIK 10 WAS A SUCCESS, AS WAS THE BIO-SENSOR INFORMATION FROM THE SPACE SUIT SHE TRAVELED IN.

ZVEZDOCHKA = Russian for "Little Star"

Sputnik 10/
Korabl-Sputnik 5
March 25, 1961
T-minus 8 years,
3 months, 25 days
Flight duration:
1 hour, 46 minutes
Zvezdochka ("Little Star")
orbits once with a dummy
cosmonaut

35

Vostok 1
April 12, 1961
Flight duration:
1 hour, 48 minutes
Altitude: 203 miles/327 km
Yuri Gagarin becomes
the first person to orbit
the earth.

True, though not the way you and he may be thinking! Gagarin's actually south of **ARGENTINA!** (Hey, it was dark, and he was busy...)

GAGARIN IS PULLING 8 G—The force of re-entry + gravity is pushing his eyeballs into his skull!

41

KCHAK

WHUMP!

OOF!

DON'T BE AFRAID!

I'M ONE OF YOURS...a SOVIET!

I HAVE COME FROM SPACE.

Mercury-Redstone 3/
Freedom 7:
May 5, 1961
T-Minus 8 Years,
2 Months, 15 Days
Flight duration:
15 minutes, 22 seconds
Altitude: 116 miles/
187 km. (Suborbital)
Alan Shepard, first
American in space

DON'T WORRY -- *Stormy didn't drive from California to Alabama. That's a* **RENTED** *T-Bird he picked up at the airport...Stormy always drove T-Birds!*

LEM = Lunar Excursion Module, later shortened to LM

LUNAR ORBIT RENDEZVOUS

50

CHECK THE FLIGHT-OPERATIONS MANUAL **NOW**.

GET THE **ENGINEERS** IN HERE **NOW**!

UH... **CANCEL** THAT PHONE CALL, JOHN. MAYBE **NEXT** TIME AROUND.

WHAT DO WE HAVE?

SEGMENT **51**, MAX.

DAMN. THE LANDING BAG **DEPLOYED** PREMATURELY?!

THIS IS FRIENDSHIP 7, BROADCASTING IN THE **BLIND** TO THE **MERCURY NETWORK**. 1, 2, 3, 4, 5. THIS IS MERCURY FRIENDSHIP 7. OUT.

THIS IS **WOOMERA CAPCOM**, READING YOU LOUD AND CLEAR.

SO THE **HEAT SHIELD'S** LOOSE.

NOT GOOD.

CAPCOM = Capsule Communicator = an astronaut on the ground, and the only person who talks directly with the astronaut in flight.

WOOMERA = A city in Australia--CAPCOMs were stationed all over the world for orbital missions. (P.S. Look up the meaning of "woomera"!)

THIS IS FRIENDSHIP 7. SXXKXSSSX HAVING **NO** TROUBLE AT ALL **EATING**, VERY GOOD.

OKAY, YOUR **MISSION RULES** SAY GET RID OF THE **RETRO-ROCKETS** ONCE THEY'VE FIRED, RIGHT?

RIGHT -- IF THERE'S ANY **FUEL** IN 'EM WHEN HE HITS THE **ATMOSPHERE**... EVEN A **LITTLE** BIT...

...BOOM.

REENTRY WILL BE SHORT, FIERY, AND **FATAL**.

OKAY...

...WON'T **HAPPEN**. THE FUEL ALWAYS BURNS **COMPLETELY**.

ARE YOU...?

SO WE LEAVE THE RETRO-ROCKETS **ON**...THAT'LL HOLD THE **HEAT SHIELD** IN PLACE.

WE HAVE MISSION RULES FOR A **REASON**, MAX.

"BELIEVE IT, FLIGHT."

I CAN SEE THE BRILLIANT BLUE HORIZON COMING UP BEHIND ME; APPROACHING SUNRISE. OVER.

ROGER, FRIENDSHIP 7. YOU ARE VERY LUCKY.

YOU'RE RIGHT, MAN. THIS IS **BEAUTIFUL**.

3rd, AND LAST, ORBIT

FRIENDSHIP 7. WE ARE RECOMMENDING THAT YOU LEAVE THE **RETRO-PACKAGE** ON THROUGH THE ENTIRE **REENTRY**.

THIS IS **FRIENDSHIP 7**. WHAT IS THE **REASON** FOR THIS? DO YOU HAVE ANY **REASON**? OVER.

NOT AT THIS TIME...

...THIS IS THE **JUDGMENT OF FLIGHT**.

55

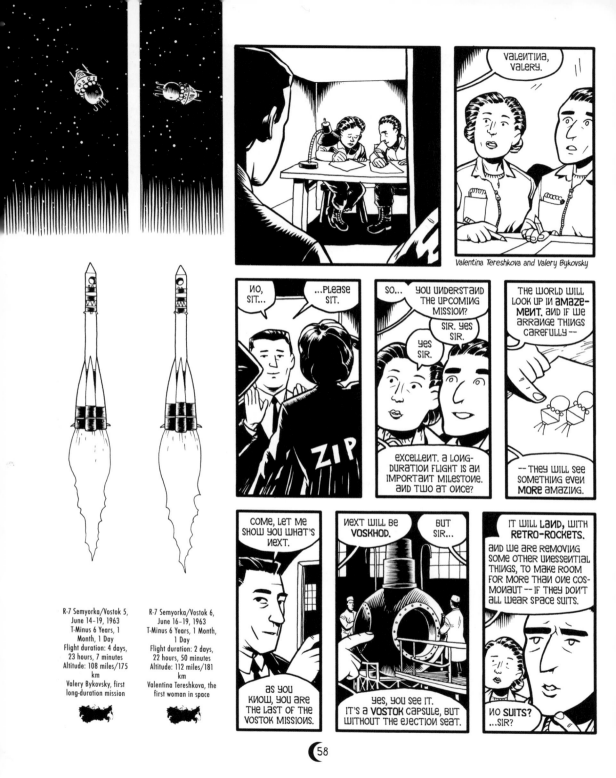

Valentina Tereshkova and Valery Bykovsky

R-7 Semyorka/Vostok 5,
June 14–19, 1963
T-Minus 6 Years, 1
Month, 1 Day
Flight duration: 4 days,
23 hours, 7 minutes
Altitude: 108 miles/175
km
Valery Bykovsky, first
long-duration mission

R-7 Semyorka/Vostok 6,
June 16–19, 1963
T-Minus 6 Years, 1 Month,
1 Day
Flight duration: 2 days,
22 hours, 50 minutes
Altitude: 112 miles/181
km
Valentina Tereshkova, the
first woman in space

"DO NOT WORRY. YOU, MY EAGLES, WILL BOTH HAVE THEM."

"AND OUR LEADERS -- AND THE WHOLE WORLD -- WILL BE AMAZED BY YOUR FLIGHT."

HOUSTON-NASA-1963

...NEED A STATEMENT, AND NEED IT BAD! THE SOVIETS HAVE TWO SPACECRAFT UP AT ONCE!

WELL, THEY ALREADY DID THAT A YEAR AGO, SO WHAT'S THE BIG DEAL?

BECAUSE THEY DID A RENDEZVOUS.

AND WE DON'T EVEN HAVE THE FIRST GEMINI MISSION GOING UP UNTIL NEXT YEAR!

MERCURY had one astronaut on board; Gemini would have two. And then...Apollo!

AND WE NEED A STATEMENT FOR THE PRESS!

OH, FOR GOD'S SAKE, SHORTY, WHAT ARE YOU TALKING ABOUT?

MAX, WHY DONTCHA GO AHEAD? I'LL SEE YOU IN THE CONFERENCE ROOM IN A MINUTE.

GRUMBLE GRIPE...

IT WAS A TRICK, SHORTY -- BYKOVSKY AND TERESKOVA DIDN'T RENDEZVOUS.

LOOK --

-- HERE'S A SIMPLIFIED ENGINEERING DRAWING OF THE GEMINI CAPSULE. FROM THE TOP, IT LOOKS LIKE THREE CIRCLES.

FROM THE BOTTOM, ONE BIG CIRCLE, AND FROM THE SIDE ...LIKE THIS.

C.C. is drawing something called an "orthographic projection."

SO IF YOU ONLY GET A 2-D VIEW OF SOMETHING, YOU DON'T GET THE WHOLE PICTURE.

AND IF THINGS ARE FAR AWAY -- LIKE SPACECRAFT IN ORBIT -- IT'S AS IF YOU ONLY GET THE VIEW THROUGH ONE SIDE OF THE BOX. SO...

...THAT'S THE SOVIET "RENDEZVOUS."

4 MILES APART

LOOKS GREAT FROM DOWN HERE, BUT IT AIN'T REAL.

I GOTTA SAY, TWO MANNED SPACECRAFT LAUNCHED TWO DAYS APART IS PRETTY GOOD, THOUGH.

59

America was hostile territory in 1965!

It is a Russian tradition for travelers to sit and compose themselves for a few minutes before a long journey.

Q: Why the empty seat? A: Voskhod 1 carried three cosmonauts ... if they didn't need space suits! But this time Alexei's going to need his!

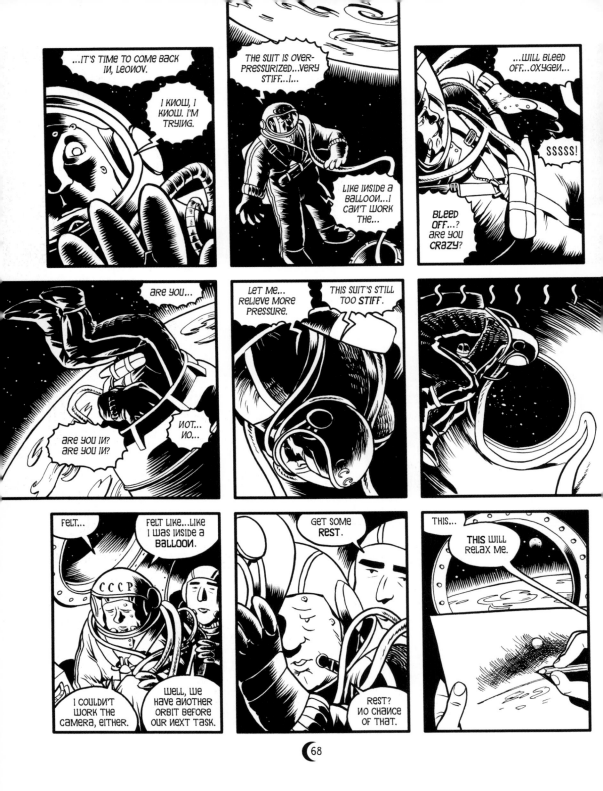

ENOUGH!

FIRST...

EVERYBODY SIT DOWN.

WHAT IS OUR STATUS?

THE AUTOMATIC RE-ENTRY SYSTEM HAS FAILED, AND WE CAN'T, WELL...

UNDERSTOOD.

HAND ME THAT HEADSET, PLEASE.

...ONE MORE ORBIT TO PREPARE THE MANUAL RETRO-ROCKETS, AND CHECK VOSKHOD'S ATTITUDE.

IT WILL TAKE YOU EXTRA TIME, SO YES, YOU'LL OVERSHOOT THE LANDING SITE.

DON'T WORRY, ALEXEI...

"...IT WILL BE FINE."

WELL, THE CHIEF DESIGNER WAS **RIGHT**...

KRK--

WE OVERSHOT THE LANDING SITE FROM OUR MISSION PROFILE!

PLENTY OF WOOD OUT THERE, THOUGH -- TOMORROW WE'LL MAKE A CAMPFIRE.

IT WILL KEEP US WARM, AND GUIDE THE RESCUE HELICOPTER.

BUT TONIGHT? WELL...

...NOT AS COLD AS SPACE AT LEAST...AND FRESH AIR!

RRR

HMM...

...AND VISITORS.

OWOOO

OWOOO

71

T-MINUS 4 YEARS, 3 MONTHS, 27 DAYS

...NO, NO...

...WE **CONGRATULATE** THE SOVIETS ON THEIR SPECTACULAR SUCCESS.

IT'S A **REMARKABLE** ACHIEVEMENT.

HOW DOES THIS CHANGE THE PLANS FOR GEMINI 3?

NO CHANGE. JOHN AND GUS ARE GONNA FLY THE MISSION THEY TRAINED FOR, WHICH IS TO CHECK OUT THEIR SPACECRAFT.

THEY'LL MAKE SURE IT'S READY FOR SOMETHING **BIG** IN GEMINI 4.

GEMINI = John Young and Gus Grissom

HERE ARE SOME SUPPLIES!

AW...

SOMETHING **BIG? WHAT?!**

THANKS BOYS. THAT'S ALL.

WE **DO** HAVE A **SURPRISE,** DON'T WE?

WE'LL HAVE TO COME UP WITH ONE.

SPACE TASK GROUP'S NEW HEADQUARTERS—HOUSTON, TEXAS

EMINI 4

EVA

GENTLEMEN, WE WERE PLANNING A "MINI EVA" SCHEDULED FOR YOUR GEMINI 4 FLIGHT.

BUT IN LIGHT OF RECENT EVENTS, WE THINK IT PRUDENT TO REEVALUATE THE SITUATION.

EVA = extravehicular activity

AND SKIS!

OWOOOOOO...

AS SUCH, THE PROFILE HAS UNDERGONE RIGOROUS AND DETAILED --

SAY IT **PLAIN,** JOE!

IF I'M NOT JUST POKING MY HEAD OUT THE **DOOR,** WHAT'LL IT **BE?**

YEAH, IF YOU'RE NOT GONNA HAVE US DO MEDICAL EXPERIMENTS, TESTS, AND OTHER ASSORTED JUNK...

...THEN WHAT?

YOU'LL GET SOME **NEW** ASSORTED JUNK.

BUT ED'S GONNA GET A NEW SUIT, AND A **GUN.**

Ed White: Pilot

Jim McDivitt: Command pilot

72

GUN? WHAT FOR?

HECK, LEONOV AND BELYAYEV HAVE LANDED, RIGHT? NO NEED FOR WEAPONS!

HA HA HA HA

VERY FUNNY.

SO, ANYWAY, THE NEW SUIT HAS 18 LAYERS, TO PROTECT AGAINST MICROMETEORITES AND EXTREME COLD.

AS FOR THE "GUN," YOU WANTED US TO SAY IT PLAIN, SO I DIDN'T CALL IT A "HANDHELD MANEUVERING UNIT."

IT FIRES COMPRESSED AIR, NOT BULLETS.

EVA

"IT'LL LET YOU MOVE AROUND --

" -- EQUAL AND OPPOSITE REACTION, AND ALL THAT."

KHOP!

CHOP!

COLONEL LEONOV! HELLO!

OK. IT'S ABOUT 9 KM TO THE HELICOPTER. ARE YOU UP FOR SOME SKIING?

SIGH

OY.

WE'VE JUST BEEN AROUND THE WORLD A FEW TIMES... WHAT'S A FEW MORE KILOMETERS?

"LET'S JUST GET OUT OF HERE."

00:04:29:28 GET

GEMINI 4, KKKKKKXXXX HAWAII CAPCOM. WHAT KXXX YOUR STATUS NOW? KXXX

ABOUT READY TO START GETTING OUT.

OK.

00:04:29:28 = 0 days, 4 hours, 29 minutes, 28 seconds
GET = GROUND ELAPSED TIME = time since liftoff

...I'M SEPARATING FROM THE SPACECRAFT.

WHY ARE YOU SO OVER-DRESSED, BLONDIE?

YOU'D THINK IT WAS COLD OUT THERE OR SOMETHING!

OK, YOU'RE RIGHT IN FRONT, ED. YOU LOOK BEAUTIFUL.

I...I...

Titan II/Gemini 4
June 3, 1965
T-Minus 4 Years,
1 Month, 17 Days
Flight duration: 4 days,
1 hour, 56 minutes
Jim McDivitt, Ed White

73

Titan II/Gemini 5:
September 21–29, 1965
T-Minus 3 Years, 9
Months, 29 Days
Flight duration: 7 days,
22 hours, 55 minutes
Motto: "8 Days or Bust"
for this 120-orbit flight
Gordon Cooper and
Charles Conrad

Titan II/Gemini 7:
December 4–18, 1965
T-Minus 3 Years, 7
Months, 16 Days
Flight duration: 13
days, 18 hours, 35
minutes
(enough time to
complete a lunar
expedition)
Frank Borman and
Jim Lovell, who both
brought books along

Titan II/Gemini 6A:
December 15–16, 1965
T-Minus 3 Years, 7
Months, 5 Days
Flight duration: 1 day,
1 hours, 51 minutes
Rendezvous with
Gemini 7
Wally Schirra and Tom
Stafford

UM...WHAT DO YOU THINK, YURI?

BLONDIN, I...I DON'T KNOW.

I CAN'T SEE HOW THIS...THING...IS GOING TO BE READY BY LAUNCH DAY.

BUT WITH ALL THESE AMERICAN LAUNCHES, THE CHIEF DESIGNER MAY BE FORCED TO SAY IT IS...

"HE'S UNDER A LOT OF PRESSURE."

HAPPY BIRTHDAY, CHIEF DESIGNER.

BOYS, THIS IS MY HOME. TONIGHT IT IS JUST SERGEI.

Now you know the Chief Designer's full name -- SERGEI KOROLEV -- before anybody in the United States did!

LATER THAT EVENING...

WE HAVE GREAT WORK AHEAD OF US, AND I FEEL MAGNIFICENT.

ESPECIALLY FOR ONE GOING INTO SURGERY.

SURGERY? WHAT'S WRONG?

DO NOT WORRY, I FEEL FINE.

HE SAID ABOUT 20 YEARS.

THE DOCTOR IS A FRIEND, AND THE PROGNOSIS IS GOOD. I ASKED HIM, "HOW MUCH LONGER WILL I BE ABLE TO CONTINUE MY WORK?"

I TOLD HIM 10 YEARS WOULD BE ENOUGH!

Titan II/Gemini 8:
March 16-17, 1966
T-Minus 3 Years, 4 Months, 4 Days
Flight duration: 10 hours, 41 minutes
First manual docking with Agena-8
Neil Armstrong and Dave Scott

Titan II/Gemini 9A:
June 3-6, 1966
T-Minus 3 Years, 1 Month, 17 Days
Flight duration: 72 hours, 20 minutes
Rendezvous, Docking, and EVA
Tom Stafford and Gene Cernan

Titan II/Gemini 10: July 18-21, 1966
T-Minus 3 Years, 2 Days
Flight duration: 70 hours, 46 minutes, 39 seconds
John Young and Michael Collins

Titan II/Gemini 11:
September 12-15, 1966
T-Minus 2 Years, 10 Months, 8 Days
Flight duration: 71 hours, 17 minutes, 8 seconds
Pete Conrad and Dick Gordon

Titan II/Gemini 12:
November 11-15, 1966
T-Minus 2 Years, 8
Months, 9 Days
Flight duration: 94
hours, 34 minutes, 31
seconds
Jim Lovell and Buzz
Aldrin

YEAH, HE WAS SOME KINDA ENGINEER.

ALL THEIR GUYS TALKED ABOUT HIM, WITHOUT TELLING US HIS NAME -- SOMETIMES I WONDER IF EVEN **THEY** KNEW IT.

YOU GOTTA WONDER WHAT HE HAD UP HIS SLEEVE.

A SAD DAY...

NASA engineers and astronauts met their **SOVIET COUNTERPARTS** now and then. They all got along well -- they had a lot in common!

T-MINUS 2 YEARS, 5 MONTHS, 23 DAYS

APOLLO/SATURN 204 (AS-204) MISSION CHECKOUT

HOW ARE YA?

LAUNCH COMPLEX 34-- CAPE KENNEDY, FLORIDA

GOOD TO SEE YOU ED. HOP ON IN AND LET'S GET THIS TEST GOING.

YOU BET!

WATCH YOUR HEAD THERE, ROGER.

THANKS, ED.

ROGER CHAFFEE = Apollo 1 Lunar Module Pilot

AGE BEFORE BEAUTY, GUS.

HA.

FUNNY.

GUS GRISSOM = Apollo 1 Commander

OKAY...

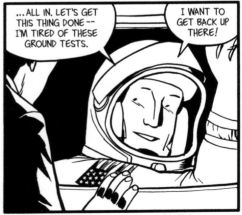

...ALL IN. LET'S GET THIS THING DONE -- I'M TIRED OF THESE GROUND TESTS.

I WANT TO GET BACK UP THERE!

ED WHITE = Apollo 1 Command and Service Module Pilot

STONY = Stu Roosa, CAPCOM for today's test

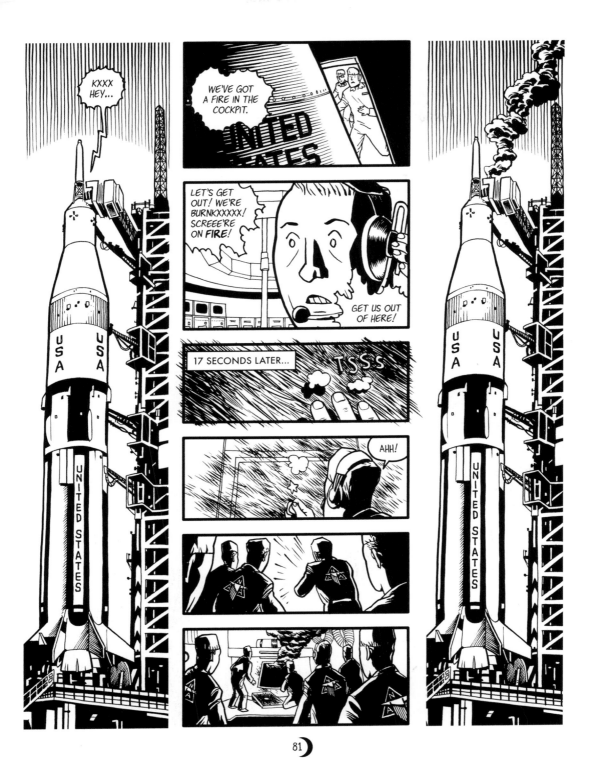

RIIING

NASA ASTRONAUT GROUP.

WHO'S THIS?

AL BEAN.

...

AL, WE'RE DOWN HERE AT THE TEST SITE.... WE'VE LOST THE CREW.

WHAT DO YOU MEAN, YOU'VE **LOST** THE CREW?

WHERE'D THEY **GO**?

GO FIND THEM -- MAYBE THEY'RE DOWN AT THE BEACH HOUSE.

The crew had a **BEACH HOUSE** near the pad, where they went over mission plans—and just hung out and barbequed and swam.

NO.

WE **LOST** THE CREW.

"I...I'D BETTER NOT DESCRIBE WHAT I SEE."

Y-YEAH.

LOOK, WE GOT GUYS OUT TESTING THAT SAME CAPSULE IN CALIFORNIA, **RIGHT NOW**.

I GOTTA MAKE SOME CALLS.

...YES, BLONDIN, I HEARD. IT IS AWFUL.

AMERICA

AND ANOTHER REASON WHY I WANT TO FLY THE NEXT MISSION.

WHAT?

YURI, YOU CAN'T BUMP KOMAROV FROM SOYUZ 1.

AND BESIDES...

...YOU'VE ALREADY FLOWN!

T-MINUS 2 YEARS, 2 MONTHS, 29 DAYS

SO? KOMAROV ALREADY FLEW AS WELL, A VOSKHOD MISSION!

YURI, LOOK. HAVEN'T WE HAD THIS CONVERSATION BEFORE?

BAIKONUR COSMODROME

YES WE HAVE. WE'RE HAVING IT AGAIN!

...

YOU REALLY **DON'T** UNDERSTAND, DO YOU, YURI?

YOU'RE A **HERO.**

YOU'RE **THE** HERO OF THE SOVIET **PEOPLE.**

AND THAT... **THAT** IS A MACHINE.

AND YOU AND I BOTH KNOW THIS NEW SOYUZ CAPSULE IS...WELL.

YES. MORE DANGEROUS THAN THE OTHERS.

THAT'S EXACTLY IT, ALEXEI.

IF IT'S TOO DANGEROUS FOR ME...

"...IT'S TOO DANGEROUS FOR VLADIMIR MIKHAILOVICH AS WELL!"

SIRS—IF THE CHIEF DESIGNER WERE ALIVE, HE WOULD NOT ALLOW...

...AND YOU CAN TELL **BREZHNEV** THAT I DON'T **CARE** IF THE PARTY DOESN'T WANT TO RISK ME!

BREZHNEV = Leonid Brezhnev, the head of the Soviet Union following Khrushchev

T-MINUS 2 YEARS, 2 MONTHS, 27 DAYS

THEY KNOW I'M RIGHT, BUT THEY WON'T LISTEN, AND THEY WON'T LET ME...

AH!

AM I STILL FLYING THIS THING, THEN?

AH, VLADIMIR, IT'S NOT THAT I **WANTED** TO BUMP YOU FROM THE FLIGHT.

YURI, I KNOW.

...BUT IF IT'S NOT ME, THEN AS BACKUP YOU WOULD BE GOING UP IN...

...

BESIDES, YOU ARE MY MDSM...

MDSM is the Soviet equivalent to NASA's CAPCOM

"...YOU WILL BE WITH ME THE WHOLE TIME!"

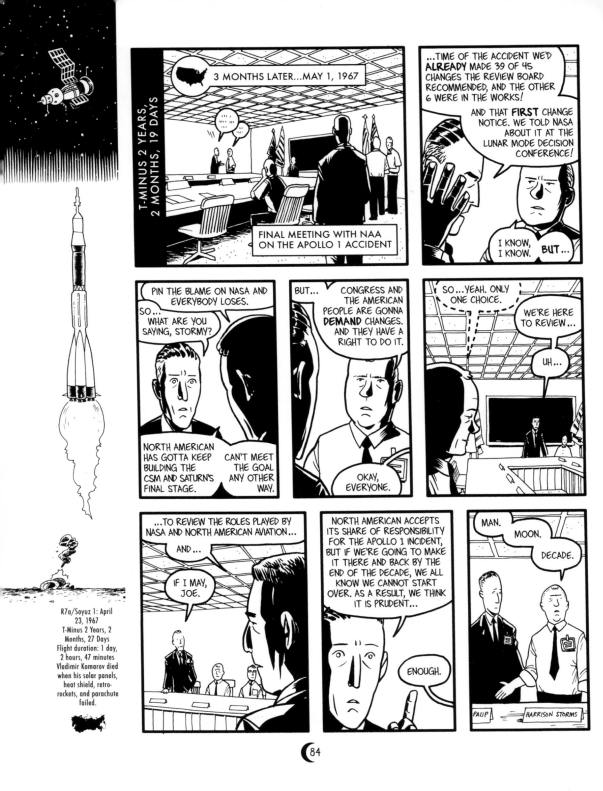

R7a/Soyuz 1: April 23, 1967
T-Minus 2 Years, 2 Months, 27 Days
Flight duration: 1 day, 2 hours, 47 minutes
Vladimir Komarov died when his solar panels, heat shield, retro-rockets, and parachute failed.

AND SO IT WENT, UNTIL...

C'MON, WAKE UP, C.C.

HUH?

WE GOTTA GET OVER TO THE CONFERENCE ROOM.

THERE'S NEWS.

T-MINUS 11 MONTHS

ALL UP

...AND CIA INTELLIGENCE SAYS THE SOVIETS WILL ORBIT THE MOON IN LATE 1968.

WHERE DO THEY GET **THAT**, GEORGE? THE RUSSIANS HAVEN'T LAUNCHED A COSMONAUT FOR... I DON'T KNOW HOW LONG!

SINCE THE **KOMAROV** ACCIDENT, AT LEAST!

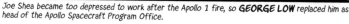

*Joe Shea became too depressed to work after the Apollo 1 fire, so **GEORGE LOW** replaced him as head of the Apollo Spacecraft Program Office.*

DOESN'T MATTER WHERE THEY GOT IT. INTELLIGENCE SAYS THEIR NEXT ZOND FLIGHT WILL BE **MANNED**.

SO WHAT DO **WE** HAVE?

ZOND = "probe." The first Zond missions were robots.

ALL **WE** HAVE IS THE CSM, AND...

AND WE HAVE THE SATURN V. WHICH WE'VE NEVER STUCK AN ASTRONAUT ON TOP OF...

CSM

AND WE HAVE HUGE COM- MITTEES THAT TAKE SIX MONTHS TO DECIDE HOW MUCH VELCRO WE CAN USE, AND...

...AND WHERE WE CAN STICK IT!

AND NO **LM.**

AND NO SOFTWARE FOR THE LM LANDING COMPUTER.

DEKE SLAYTON = one of the original Mercury 7, and now NASA's director of flight crew operations. He decided who flew what mission.

OKAY, FINE.

WE DO HAVE GUIDANCE AND NAVIGATION COMPUTERS, THOUGH,...

...AND WE WEREN'T GOING TO LAND ANYWAY. AT LEAST NOT **YET.**

BUT, WE'RE OUT OF **TIME.** IT'S "ALL UP" TESTING FROM NOW ON -- WE TRY A LOT OF THINGS AT ONCE, AND LEARN FASTER.

SO, WHAT'S THE CURRENT MISSION PROFILE FOR APOLLO 8?

TEST THE LM IN EARTH ORBIT.

C'MON, CHRIS. APOLLO 7 **ALREADY TESTED** THE CSM IN ORBIT, AND...

CSM

...WE. DON'T. HAVE. AN **LM!**

I'LL SAY IT AGAIN: **ALL UP.**

ORBIT THE **MOON.**

THIS YEAR -- 1968.

USA

"...CALL IT THE X MISSION."

"THE X MISSION?"

GENE KRANZ *took over from Chris Kraft as Mission Control's "Flight."*

Frank Borman: Commander (CDR)
Jim Lovell: Command Module Pilot (CMP)
Bill Anders: Lunar Module Pilot (LMP)

"SHE THOUGHT WE WERE GOING TO ACAPULCO. GUESS I'D BETTER TELL HER THERE'S A CHANGE IN OUR HOLIDAY PLANS."

CHRISTMAS?

HICKAM AIR FORCE BASE— HONOLULU, HAWAII

SIR, YES SIR.

OKAY, YOUNG MAN. WHAT HAVE YOU GOT TO SAY?

WELL...

...IN THIS MISSION...

...WE WILL LEARN HOW TO RIDE A SATURN V.

WE WILL LEARN WHAT IT MEANS TO LEAVE EARTH'S GRAVITATIONAL FIELD.

WE WILL LEARN HOW GOOD OUR RADAR TRACKING AND ONBOARD GUIDANCE COMPUTER IS.

WE WILL LEARN HOW TO REENTER EARTH'S ATMOSPHERE FROM ANOTHER PLANET.

AND WE NEED YOU TO PICK UP THE ASTRONAUTS WHEN THEY SPLASH DOWN.

ADMIRAL JOHN McCAIN = father of future senator John McCain, who was a prisoner of war in Vietnam at the time.

ADMIRAL McCAIN, NASA REALIZES YOU'VE MADE YOUR PLANS ALREADY...

...BUT WE'RE ASKING YOU TO CHANGE THEM.

SNATCH!

APOLLO 8 ORBIT PROFILE

WE NEED YOU TO RE-DEPLOY THE UM... FLEET TO--

UH...

BEST DAMN BRIEFING I'VE EVER HAD.

GIVE MR. KRAFT AND NASA WHAT THEY WANT.

YES, SIR!

"OKAY, GUYS..."

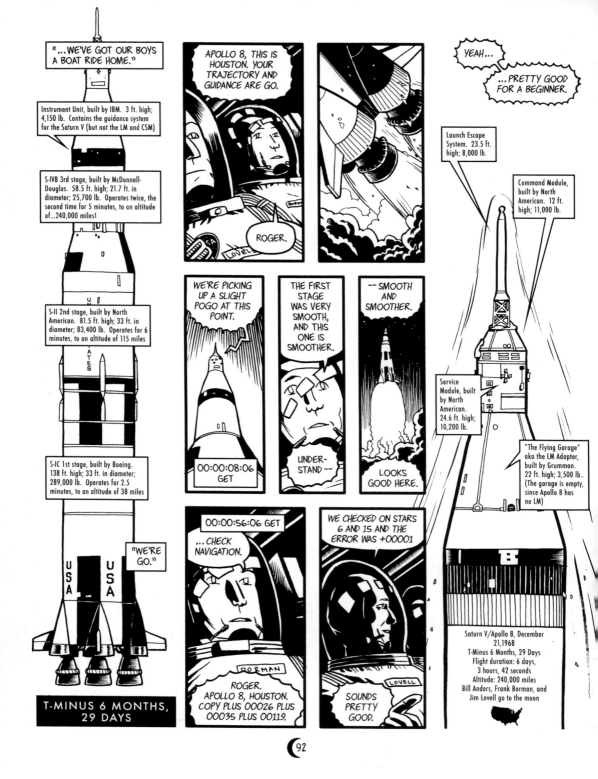

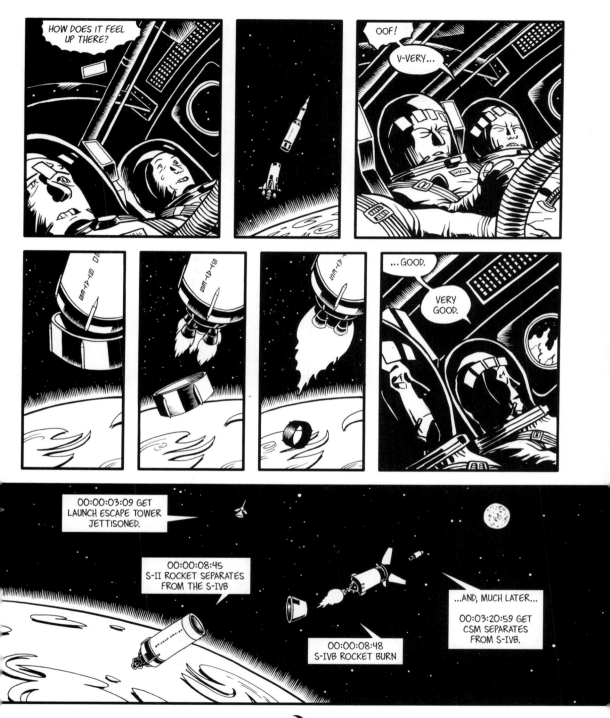

CANARIES = Canary Islands

TLI = Trans-Lunar Injection = going to the moon!

MAE WEST = Air Force pilot and astronaut nickname for a life vest (which Frank Borman mistakenly calls a raft).

CAPCOM: Michael Collins

94

SO WE WILL BE SIGNING OFF HERE, AND WE WILL BE LOOKING FORWARD TO SEEING YOU ALL AGAIN SHORTLY.

ROGER.

GOOD-BYE FROM APOLLO 8.

02:20:04:07 GET

APOLLO 8, THIS IS HOUSTON. AT 68:04 HOURS YOU ARE GO FOR LOI-1.

GO FLIGHT!

GO!

GO!

GO!

LOI-1 = Lunar Orbit Insertion 1 = the first trip around the moon

OK. APOLLO 8 IS GO.

YOU ARE RIDING THE BEST BIRD WE CAN FIND. OVER.

ROGER. IT'S A GOOD ONE.

02:20:56:06 GET

APOLLO 8, HOUSTON. TWO MINUTES UNTIL LOS.

LOS = Loss of Signal again....It doesn't matter whether there are satellites orbiting Earth, because this time, for the first time, the moon is in the way.

ROGER.

APOLLO 8, HOUSTON. ONE MINUTE TO LOS. ALL SYSTEMS GO.

SAFE JOURNEY, GUYS.

APOLLO 8, 10 SECONDS TO GO. YOU'RE GO ALL THE WAY.

THANKS A LOT, TROOPS.

WE'LL SEE YOU ON THE OTHER SIDE.

WELL, DID YOU GUYS EVER THINK THAT ONE CHRISTMAS EVE...

...YOU'D BE ORBITING THE MOON?

WELL...

...JUST HOPE WE'RE NOT DOING IT ON NEW YEAR'S.

HEH HEH HEH

96

OHHH, THAT'S A BEAUTIFUL SHOT.

YOU **SURE** WE GOT IT NOW?

YES...

...IT'LL COME UP AGAIN, I THINK, RIGHT OVER...

AW...

OKAY...

HA HA HA HA HA HA

...BACK TO YOUR RESIDUALS. PROCEED.

LATITUDE, MINUS 06269, LONGITUDE OVER TWO, MINUS 78954, ATTITUDE, PLUS 00152.

APOLLO 8, THIS IS HOUSTON. OVER.

LOUD AND CLEAR, HOUSTON.

OKAY, FRANK, I'LL BRING YOU UP-TO-DATE ON A COUPLE OF THINGS.

THE P27 WHICH WE WILL BE SENDING YOU IS A STATE VECTOR UPDATE GOING TO THE LM SLOT...

...AND WE'D LIKE TO -- AS PER PLAN -- TO TRANSFER THAT TO THE CSM SLOT...

...PRIOR TO DOING YOUR VERB 47, ENTER, MANUALLY SELECT POO AND WAIT FOR THE COMPUTER ACTIVITY LIGHT TO GO OUT.

ROGER, ROGER, WE COPY.

SUCCESSFUL

USSR: N1-L3: February
21, 1969
T-Minus 149 Days
Flight duration: 69
seconds, ending in an
explosion

"THE CSM'S COMING IN FROM CALIFORNIA ON THE SUPER GUPPY THIS WEEK."

UNITED STATES

• CSM flown in from Downey, California on the Super Guppy (Look it up! What a great plane!)

• LM from Bethpage, New York, also traveling by Super Guppy

• Space suits from Dover, Delaware

• Saturn V, shipped by barge from Huntsville, Alabama

SOVIET UNION

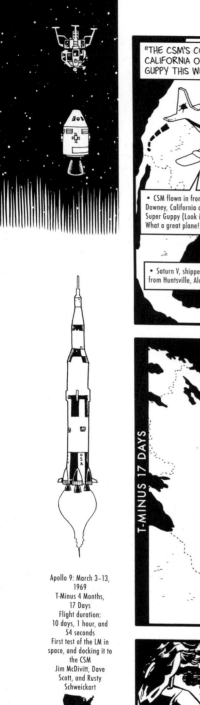

T-MINUS 17 DAYS

Apollo 9: March 3-13, 1969
T-Minus 4 Months, 17 Days
Flight duration: 10 days, 1 hour, and 54 seconds
First test of the LM in space, and docking it to the CSM
Jim McDivitt, Dave Scott, and Rusty Schweickart

Apollo 10: May 18-26, 1969
T-Minus 63 Days
Flight duration: 8 days, 3 minutes, and 23 seconds, including more than 2 days in lunar orbit
The dress rehearsal to check out the landing site on the Sea of Tranquility.
Tom Stafford, John Young, and Gene Cernan

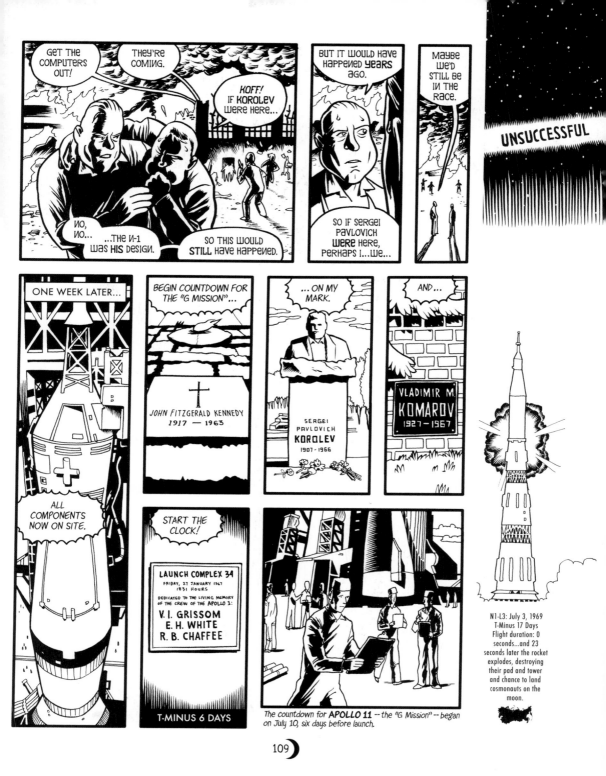

FREDO HAISE = Buzz Aldrin's backup Lunar Module Pilot for Apollo 11. His job is to prepare the spacecraft for liftoff.

CHRIS KRAFT is now Max's boss

"The Flying Garage" aka the LM Adapter

The garage is full this time—Apollo 11 is carrying "Eagle" to the moon

FLIP FLIP FLIP FLIP FLIP FLIP FLI

STATES

...AND THAT'S 417 -- GIVE OR TAKE. YOUR TURN TO FLIP THOSE SWITCHES, GUYS.

THANKS, FREDO.

HERE YOU GO, GÜNTER.

It was tradition for astronauts to give "Pad Leader" Günter Wendt a **PARTING GIFT**, since he was the last person they saw on Earth.

CATCH ME SOMETHING WHILE I'M UP THERE.

JA, VILL DO, MIKE.

Michael Collins and Günter fished together.

CLICK

ZRT

PSST

SHUN-KLIK

UNITED STATES

The Saturn V engines all **PIVOT** ("gimbal") as the guidance computer hunts around to correct the flight direction. As Mike Collins said, "it was steering like crazy, like a nervous, novice driver in a narrow alleyway."

EQUIGRAVISPHERE = the point where the Earth's and the moon's gravity balance out. If you didn't want to come home, you could stop and balance there forever!

In 1969, Italian TV was only broadcast in **BLACK-AND-WHITE**.

DSKY = Display/keyboard for the AGC
AGC = Apollo Guidance Computer, which all the astronauts loved...and relied on.

OMNI = Omni-directional antenna, which Buzz and Neil can point wherever they want.

117

The **1202** and **1201 ALARMS** happened because Buzz had the landing and rendezvous computers both running (just in case), so the AGC's memory—barely big enough to hold four seconds of an MP3—struggled to keep up.

DID ALL OF THIS REALLY HAPPEN?

July 20, 1969

Yes...mostly! However, about 400,000 men and women worked on Mercury, Gemini, and Apollo—to show them all would've meant having more than 3,000 people on each page! So C.C. and Max are based on real NASA engineers Caldwell C. Johnson and Max Faget, but in our story they not only play their own parts, but also stand in for many other engineers and technical people as well. Similarly, we have Harrison Storms of North American Aviation say and do some things on behalf of other private contractors. And just like in the United States, thousands of people worked on the Soviet space program. Sergei Korolev was so pivotal, though, that he almost always spoke for himself. But just so you know, to make *T-Minus* we

One small step: Neil Armstrong walks on the moon, the first of only 12 to do so.

sometimes had to create some parts (scenes!) from scratch, imagining what people might have done,

thought, or said so we could tell you the story more clearly.

DIG DEEPER

NASA's History Division has created sites called "Apollo Lunar Surface Journal" (*history.nasa.gov/alsj*) and "Apollo Flight Journal" which give detailed accounts of what the astronauts saw and did on their way to and from the moon, and while they walked and drove around on it. It's a work in progress, but the text, videos, and pictures that are there already are tremendous. The NASA Library at their headquarters in Washington DC has made many great publications on all aspects of space exploration, and the folks there were very helpful to us as well.

As great as it was to discover interesting stuff in libraries and book stores, reading mission transcripts (*www.jsc. nasa.gov/history/mission_ trans/mission_transcripts. htm*), oral histories (*www.jsc. nasa.gov/history/oral_his tories/oral_histories.htm*) and talking to people was the real thrill of making this book. We owe special thanks to astronauts Buzz Aldrin, Neil Armstrong, and Alan Bean for sharing their expertise, support, and encouragement.

Finally, if you want to read more comics about the space race, you can find out about the first dog in space, and Korolev as well, from Nick Abadzis' book *Laika* (New York: First Second, 2007). And you'll meet Ham, the first chimpanzee to fly in space, in Jim Vining's book, *First in Space* (Portland, OR: Oni Press, 2007).

The stack of books we read to make this one is more than ten feet tall, so there's much more for you to read, too. For a full list of the things we consulted to make this book, visit *gt-labs.com/tminus.html*.

AND NOW, BACK TO C.C., ON THE GOOD EARTH...

THERE'S MORE TO SEE, MORE TO READ!

Chaikin, Andrew. *A Man on the Moon: The Voyages of the Apollo Astronauts* (New York: Viking Adult, 1994).

This book, the basis for the HBO Series *From the Earth to the Moon*, is long and complete, but it won't feel long. Since the book you're holding is only about the race through Apollo 11, we promised ourselves we would stop once we finished that chapter. But, we couldn't stop reading once we started. You won't be able to put it down either.

———

Collins, Michael. *Carrying the Fire: An Astronaut's Journeys* (New York: Cooper Square Press, 2001).

Our favorite book by an astronaut—others come close, but this is the best.

———

Gray, Mike. *Angle of Attack: Harrison Storms and the Race to the Moon* (New York: W. W. Norton, 1992).

The only book on Stormy that we know of. It reads like a mystery, even though you already know how it's going to end.

———

Harford, James. *Korolev: How One Man Masterminded the Soviet Drive to Beat America to the Moon* (New York: John Wiley & Sons, Inc., 1997).

There's a longer biography of Korolev out there, but it's written

in Russian, so we couldn't read it. Korolev lived a hard life, and if he hadn't died prematurely, the space race might have been a photo-finish, and then shifted immediately to one focused on a Mars landing.

———

Scott, David and Alexei Leonov, with Christine Toomey. *Two Sides of the Moon* (New York: St. Martin's Press, 2004).

Alexei Leonov's first person account of his spacewalk and what happened afterward is the best part of this book...at least for us. He and David Scott tell so many great stories, though, that you may find a different favorite.

———

Spacecraft Films. *Apollo 8: Leaving the Cradle, Apollo 10: The Dress Rehearsal, Apollo 11: Men on the Moon, and Mission to the Moon.*

These DVDs compile NASA films and other video to give you a sense of what it was really like to be on a trip to the moon. If you're expecting iMAX, you'll be disappointed, but remember that there was no such thing as iMAX in the 1960s. There were no HDTVs or cell phones, Internet, or PCs either. In fact, *Mission to the Moon* will show you how they made computers back then, when it was all very new. Amazing! Spacecraft Films has produced cool DVDs on the Mercury and Gemini programs as well.

Murray, Charles and Catherine Bly Cox. *Apollo: The Race to the Moon* (New York: Simon and Schuster, 1989).

This book gives the most complete and readable account of the science and engineering that went into building the first spacecraft. If these stories won't get you interested in studying math, or taking apart your bicycle to see how it works, nothing will.

———

Smith, Andrew. *Moondust: In Search of the Men Who Fell to Earth* (New York: Fourth Estate, 2005).

If you want to know what it was like to grow up during the space race, and want to find out what the moonwalkers are doing now, this book will tell you. It's clear Smith had a great time writing it as well!

———

In the Shadow of the Moon. Directed by David Sington and featuring astronauts Buzz Aldrin, Alan Bean, Eugene Cernan, Michael Collins, Charlie Duke, Jim Lovell, Edgar D. Mitchell, Harrison Schmitt, Dave Scott, and John Young (THINKFilm, 2007).

Rare footage and candid discussions of what it was like to train on, fly in, and land the Apollo spacecraft. Very cool.

Remember *EOR*? It's Earth Orbit Rendezvous.

ALEXEI LEONOV flew the Soviet half of Apollo-Soyuz, so the USA + USSR scene you saw C.C. draw on page 62 came true...sort of.